MANCHESTER
AIRPORT

Ian Howarth

Airlife
England

ACKNOWLEDGEMENTS

I would like to thank many people for their help in the production of this book. The Aviation Society, in particular Peter Hampson for his encouragement and practical help in terms of airside transport etc. The Bird Control Section, Lee Woodhead, Emyr Evans, John Davies for the countless favours.

In addition the invaluable contributions from Lee Collins, Chris Walkden and Emma Terry have been greatly appreciated.

The majority of the book has been photographed on Fuji RDP 135 by Canon F1 Cameras and Canon Lenses. The balance being shot by Hasselblad cameras on to Kodak EPN 120.

Ian Howarth

First published in the UK in 1993
by Airlife Publishing Ltd.

British Library Cataloguing in Publication Data
A catalogue record for this book is
available from the British Library.

ISBN 1 85310 387 X

Printed by Livesey Ltd, Shrewsbury.

Airlife Publishing Ltd

101 Longden Road, Shrewsbury SY3 9EB

INTRODUCTION

Success in aviation is not simply about being the largest business or the fastest growing airport. Success is also measured by the quality of customer service and commitment to be the best.

For Manchester Airport, this was proved when in 1992 it was voted 'Best UK Airport' — for the second consecutive year — by Britain's travel trade.

Manchester Airport is the country's most accessible airport, the region's motorway system is the most comprehensive in the UK. Air services feed the Manchester hub from 17 towns and cities, more than any other airport. Some shorter routes now see over 50 per cent of passengers transferring on to connecting flights at Manchester. Over 400 buses and coaches a day link destinations throughout the Airport's catchment. From Leeds and Liverpool to York and Newcastle, coaches regularly transport families to the Airport to link with their flights to their chosen holiday destination.

1992 saw a further link in the creation of a total transport hub. A stunning rail station is the centrepiece of a £26 million investment in new rail facilities that will connect Manchester directly to more than 40 points on the British Rail network — 24 hours a day. The Airport is committed to achieving a substantial increase in public transport usage through enhanced rail and coach services.

For the region, Manchester Airport is a crucial link to the world marketplace. Many organisations have chosen their location within close proximity to the Airport to ensure that they are well connected with their suppliers, clients and contacts worldwide. The Airport has been identified as a main driving force behind the regional economy and a generator of business opportunities. Many major airlines' and tour operators' achievements have been inextricably linked to the Airport's development. Manchester Airport plays a major role in stimulating inbound tourism with an intense marketing programme directed at overseas travel agents and tour operators.

The World Freight Terminal is a major asset to the area. It is the only fully integrated cargo centre in Britain, the crossroad for a mesmerising range of merchandise — tropical fish, silicone chips and wings for British Aerospace.

Manchester Airport achieves success through delivering high quality services to its customers. Airlines large and small share in the success of the Manchester hub. From New York to Larnaca, Copenhagen to Dundee, passengers across our network transferred at Manchester in ever increasing numbers. From many domestic points a connection via Manchester provides the first and fastest connection to destinations as diverse as Milan and Toronto. In 1991, Manchester was one of very few major world airports to generate an increase in passenger volumes with a record 10.9 million passengers using the Airport.

Our region needs presence and identity upon the world stage, a symbol that reflects its size, status and immense potential. The Airport, increasingly, fulfils this role within its day to day business. It attracts the global attention of influential travellers who otherwise may never have visited the region. How soon before their favoured transfer point becomes a convention centre or as a choice for investment? With a first class world airport at its heart, the North West's credentials as a major European business centre are all the more credible.

Manchester Airport will continue to provide impetus to the regional and, indeed, national economy. The Airport is committed to investment and Terminal 2 — the biggest single construction in the North of England — signals to the world our enthusiasm and determination to keep Manchester at the forefront of international trade.

Manchester Airport — Best UK Airport.

G. W. Thompson, OBE
Chief Executive

In preparation for its departure to Milan, an Alitalia Airbus A300 is seen here in the process of refuelling and being loaded with baggage. This aircraft had just brought in the Italian team for the World Student Games in Sheffield.

Opposite: A first for Manchester, an American Airlines MD11 flight AA54, the world's latest and largest wide bodied trijet on its maiden trans-Atlantic crossing. 200ft 10in long, 169ft 10in wide from wing tip to wing tip, 57ft 11in high at the tail the MD11 can carry 250 passengers and is powered by three General Electric CF6-80C2DIF engines.

Below: A GB Airways B737–200 awaits clearance from Air Traffic Control on Runway 24 to commence its journey to Gibraltar.

Right: Lufthansa's charter airline Condor is pictured here on a visit to Manchester. It was chartered by Volkswagen to bring a party of German dealers over to meet their British counterparts. The aircraft is a brand new B767.

Below: Seen here on 'push back' is an Iberia Airbus 320, bound for Barcelona, host city of the 1992 Olympics.

Opposite: Newcomer to Manchester, Poland's national carrier LOT commences a weekly Manchester to Warsaw service with a new build B737–500 replacing the Soviet-built TU134 and TU154 used in previous years.

Below: An El Al B767 about to touch down. In the background is an old Trident aircraft used for training purposes by Manchester Airport's Fire Service and the ILS Glide Slope Aerial which provides height information for poor weather landings.

Opposite: A Viva Air B737 parked up on Pier B, its bright livery reminiscent of the sun and sea, perfect for a charter airline. The colour scheme was designed by Spanish school children!

Below: As the early morning mist rises a Monarch Airlines B757 taxis to the runway. In the background an Airship used for aerial advertising is tethered to its mast.

Right: The Spanish airline Air Europa's B737s regularly fly into and out of Manchester.

Below: The magnificence of the Boeing 747 is captured here, close up on a long lens. This is a Saudia flight on diversion from Heathrow.

Opposite: Flight KL 156 B737–400 operated by Royal Dutch Airlines en route to Amsterdam.

Below: The large and the small. As this British Airways B767 rotates it reveals the southside of the Airport where business and leisure aircraft are based.

Opposite: Manchester or Majorca? Spanish charter airline Spanair, based in Palma de Mallorca have the monopoly of Pier B stands on a busy Saturday night in June.

Below: Enthusiasts on top of the multi-storey car park look on as the arrival of a Delta Air Lines Airbus from Atlanta creates frantic activity on the apron.

Opposite: The daily activity of an international airport: as American Airlines' 312AA B767 223ER to JFK, New York taxis out Aer Lingus's B737–500 takes to the air, bound for Paris.

Below: During its long stay this Qantas B747-400 is parked up on the West Apron. Before departure it will be towed back to Pier C for passengers to embark.

Opposite: A dramatic sky over Pier C where Singapore Airlines, Cathay Pacific and American Airlines have aircraft parked.

Below: A Delta TriStar taxis off Runway 24 having arrived from Atlanta.

Opposite: Military aircraft occasionally pay a fleeting visit to Manchester. Here a French Air Force C–130 Hercules departs on a navigation training flight.

Right: Full of holiday makers, this Caledonian TriStar G–BBAI rotates on its way to Larnaca, Cyprus.

Bottom: A Scandinavian Airlines System McDonnell Douglas 87 taxis by after landing. The unusual feature of this aircraft is the nose wheel skid which stops snow clogging up the nose wheel in winter.

Below: One of Manchester-based charter airline Air 2000's B757 fleet takes to the skies. Their flight prefix, AMM, is based on the Roman numerals MM which is 2000.

Below: ZS–SAV SAA B747–300 arrives in Manchester on a twice-weekly flight from Johannesburg. SAA is known as 'Springbok' like South Africa's rugby and cricket teams.

Opposite: Cathay Pacific operate a twice-weekly service from Manchester to Hong Kong. This particular flight will go via Frankfurt before continuing direct to the Far East.

Below: This dramatic angled shot of an Air Canada 767 bound for Toronto affords us with a view of the airbridges on Pier C which allow passengers to make a smooth transition from aircraft to terminal building without having to come into contact with the elements.

Right: 'Reverse thrust on, spoilers raised, lift dump active' — this British Airways 747, G–BDXH, slows on runways after touching down from Islamabad.

Below: Britannia is the largest charter airline operating from Manchester carrying over 1.5 million charter passengers through Manchester in 1991. In 1992 they celebrated 30 years as a charter airline, a great aviation achievement. Seen here, a B767 prepares for its flight to Alicante.

Opposite: Here we see a Britannia B737–200 returning from Malta. The strange vehicle on the left is an ambulift which allows wheelchair passengers to disembark in comfort when the aircraft is not parked at an airbridge.

Below: Until Christmas 1992 this shot was a daily scene, as British Airways BAC 1–11s prepared for their early take off slots to the major European cities. British Airways Manchester now operates nine B737s on their comprehensive route network from Manchester.

Opposite: Pictured is flight OK759 CSA Czechoslovakia Airlines IL62 taxi-ing towards Runway 24.

Below: Although a relative newcomer to the charter scene in 1991, Northern-based airline Airtours, have already carried over half a million passengers to their holidays. Seen here is one of their MD83 aircraft.

Opposite: Eurocypria's A320 is a new aircraft for a new airline, the charter arm of Cyprus Airways.

Below: Passengers making their way on board a Slovenian registered Adria Airways MD82 SL–ABA.

Opposite: Another large charter airline, Luton-based Monarch Airlines, base this Airbus A300 along with a fleet of B757s at Manchester.

Below: Although this B757 has Inter European Airways on its fuselage, the rest of the livery is in the colours of Air Aruba from the Caribbean.

Opposite: With its very distinctive livery, Portuguese charter airline Air Columbus regularly flies into Manchester. Pictured here is a B727–200 CS–TKB.

Below: New for 1992 with a striking livery, charter airline Excalibur chose Manchester for the delivery of their three new Airbus A320s, here is G–HAGT. Callsign is Camelot.

Right: British Airways offer twelve daily shuttle services from Manchester to London using B757s.

Bottom: TC–ACA B737–400 Istanbul Airlines arrives in Manchester on its inaugural flight from Istanbul.

Below: Pakistan International Airways operate a twice-weekly service from Manchester to Islamabad. Here is B747 AP–AYV on stand 26 with twin airbridges attached.

Opposite: New in service in the summer of 1992 this Air 2000 A320 Airbus climbs steeply into the clouds.

Below: Late in the evening an Air France B737–500 F–GINL arrives from Paris–Charles de Gaulle.

Opposite: What some would call a typical Manchester Day! A Delta Airbus from Atlanta lands in driving rain. This particular aircraft is at a transitional stage from Pan Am colours to Delta livery.

Below: Air UK B737–400 'Flagship St Francis' rotates on runway 24.

Opposite: It is easy to see from this dramatic shot of Concorde why it still pulls in the crowds. Often chartered for once-in-a-lifetime trips, Concorde is a regular visitor to Manchester.

Below: Seen here on take-off is a Singapore Airlines B747–400 'Megatop' 9V–SMF. The small hump situated about half way down the aircraft is a fairing covering an aerial for satellite telephone communications for passengers' use during the flight route from Manchester to Singapore.

Right: Air Malta flight KM201 leaves the grey skies of Manchester for sunnier climes.

Bottom: Canadian Airlines International B767–300 C–FCAV leaves Manchester for Toronto. The aircraft fleet number 636 is just visible on its nose wheel and fin tip.

Below: In preparation for an early departure to Brussels, Sabena's B737–500 flight SN616.

Opposite: Just back from Paphos, a B757–200 of Cardiff-based Inter European Airways taxi-ing towards Terminal 1B.

Right: This TAP Air Portugal B737 makes ready to depart for Lisbon. Manchester's newly refurbished Visual Control Tower can be seen in the background.

Below: Swissair's early morning flight to Zurich, SR843, an Airbus 310, taxis to runway 24.

Below: Cyprus Airways have added the smaller A320 Airbus to their fleet to supplement the A310. Here an A320 pushes back prior to departure for Larnaca.

Opposite: Lufthansa German Airlines B737–300 arrives from Frankfurt.

Below: Lufthansa LH4034 from Dusseldorf moves towards stand 23 on Pier C.

Opposite: Double take — this French registered Air Liberte MD83 is French on one side, Arabic on the other because it is operating for the Tunisian branch of the Airline!

Below: Emirates A300–600 Manchester to Dubai via Paris has a quick turn round time if the weather is good or bad.

Right: One of Manchester-based charter airline Air 2000's B757s taxis round Pier C to runway 06 for its departure to Corfu.

Below: A regular visitor to Manchester is American Transair, a charter carrier which flies to North America. Shown here is a Lockheed L–1011 TriStar — passing the Precision Approach Path Indicators, which are a landing aid to pilots. The carrier also operates Boeing 757s.

Opposite: Air Transat TriStar C–FTNB touches down on runway 24 on arrival from Toronto.

Below: In the foreground is an Aeroflot TU154 on a scheduled flight to Moscow, visible behind is a Balkan TU154 about to complete push back.

Right: A fuel strike at Larnaca airport, prompted Inter European Airlines to charter this Middle Eastern Airlines B747. IEA's B737s and B757s could not make the journey to Larnaca and back to Manchester without refuelling whereas this B747 could.

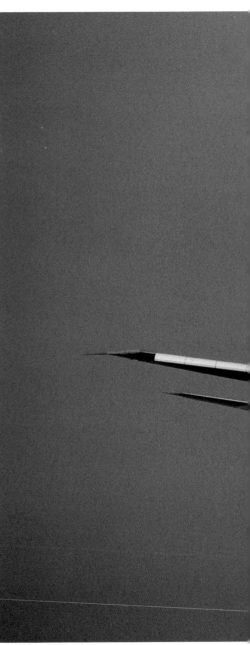

Below: A B747 outside the FLS hangar, newly repainted in the colours of Okada Air, a Nigerian airline.

Opposite: An Air Zimbabwe B767 with the more familiar sight of an Air Littoral EMB Brasilia in the foreground taxi-ing for a departure to Lyon.

When adverse weather conditions affect operations at other airports, Manchester is frequently unaffected. The Airport's wide range of facilities and ability to handle all types of aircraft often means that it is designated the number one alternative. When fog blankets the South East, a wide variety of unusual airlines from all over the world can be seen on the apron. Here are some of the more exotic aircraft visitors during one winter morning.

Opposite: A TWA B747 departs Manchester once the fog has lifted at Gatwick, now several hours late on its flight from St Louis.

Below: This British West Indies Airlines TriStar makes its way to a remote stand to wait for the fog to lift at Heathrow.

Below: A British Airways Manchester 737 taxis towards Gate 22 having arrived from Hanover.

Opposite: This hybrid liveried British Airways/ Dan Air 737 at Terminal A awaits for the airbridge to be attended.

Below: Gulf Air operate a twice weekly flight to Abu Dhabi via Frankfurt on a B767 aircraft seen here on Stand 32 of Pier C.

Opposite: All aboard an Aer Lingus Fokker 50 to Cork. The impressive new Visual Control Room can be seen in the distance.

Below: It's not all work, the crew of a Gill Air Shorts 330 pose for a publicity shot to promote the Manchester/Newcastle connection.

Right: Just after take-off, a Beech Kingair 90 G–BBVM, one of the air taxi fleet operated by Northern Executive Aviation.

Below: Manx Airlines' ATP passes the welcoming 'MANCHESTER' sign on the face of Terminal 1.

Opposite: A Fokker 50 of DLT, now renamed Lufthansa City Line, arrives in the early morning from Hamburg passing two diverted B747s on the West Apron.

Below: Loganair Shorts 360 G–WACK taxis out from Terminal A en route to Londonderry, passing Air Kilroe's General Aviation Hangar in the background.

Opposite: The National Grid Helicopter, Squirrel G–GRID, which is often based at Manchester, takes to the air for a routine check of power lines.

Right: Built locally by British Aerospace at Woodford, a British Airways ATP manoeuvres away from Terminal A for a teatime flight to Aberdeen.

Below: Suckling Airways proves that you don't have to be a giant to be a success. Husband and wife team Roy and Merlyn Suckling operate this Dornier Do228 on a daily Manchester/ Cambridge route.

Below F900 F–GJPM of Michelin taxis towards the General Aviation Terminal.

Opposite: Fresh from the Isle of Man, a Manx Shorts 360 heads for Terminal A. Opened in May 1989, Terminal A exclusively handles all Manchester's domestic traffic.

Below: One of Air Kilroe's BAe Jetstreams returns after completing another air taxi assignment.

Opposite: Base Business Airlines Jetstream parked on the south bay after an early morning arrival from Eindhoven.

Below: Business Air's Saab SF340 twice daily service arrives from Dundee.

Opposite: Passengers relax overlooking the activity on the apron.

Below: Passenger Information Boards display the worldwide destinations that can be reached from Manchester.

Right: The daily activity in the main concourse of Terminal 1B continues under Manchester's spectacular chandeliers.

AMM458	Malta	1515	Go To Passport Control	
AZ1299	Milan	1545	Go To Gate	04
BA5042	Madrid	1545	Go To Gate	03
BY459A	Palma	1550	Go To Passport Control	
EI623	Dublin	1555	Go To Gate	26
TP465	Lisbon	1555	Go To Gate	28
BA5006	Paris De Gaulle	1600	Go To Passport Control	
BA5152	Frankfurt	1600	Go To Passport Control	
BY158A	Heraklion	1600	Go To Passport Control	
EI515	Dublin	1620		
DA4270	Venice Pisa	1630	Go To Passport Control	
AIH407	Palma	1630	Go To Passport Control	
IEA570	Thessalonika	1645	Departing 1830	
BA5134	Dusseldorf	1710	Go To Passport Control	
BA119	Islamabad	1725	Go To Passport Control	
BA5020	Brussels	1725		
EI668	Zurich	1725		
EI516	Paris De Gaulle	1730		
EI618	Amsterdam	1740		

LH4135	Hamburg	1825
AIH415	Kos	1825
SK542	Copenhagen	1830
LH4057	Dusseldorf	1835
LH4083	Munich	1845
AF997	Paris De Gaulle	1850
AMM420	Larnaca	1855
BY305A	Las Palmas	1910
KL158	Amsterdam	1920
SN618	Brussels	1925
IL524	Istanbul	1935
EI517	Dublin	1955
AIH417	Las Palmas	2000
PK790	Islamabad Dubai	2100
AMM446	Thessalonika	2120
EI219	Dublin	2130
BY354A	Alicante	2140
KM203	Malta	2235
AMM484	Malta	2245

NO FLIGHT CALLS ARE MADE

cy

Passengers only
Republic of Ireland

International departures
Passport control

Passengers o

Below: A history lesson, pupils from St Matthew's RC High School, Newton Heath learn about two famous Mancunians, Captain John Alcock and Lieutenant Arthur Whitten Brown — the first men to fly non-stop across the Atlantic in 1919. This statue by Elizabeth Frink commemorates their great achievement.

Right: A rare visitor to Manchester Airport, this North Korean KCA Airlines IL 62 was here to drop off athletes for the World Student Games in Sheffield.

Below: Manchester Airport PLC has its own operations tower. Situated high above Terminal 1B's departure lounge it offers commanding views of the airfield and apron. From here the Apron Controllers liaise with ATC and allocate stands for aircraft parking.

Opposite: This newly registered YAK 42 of Lithuanian Airlines was previously part of the massive Soviet Airline Aeroflot. However, with the Soviet Union fragmenting, the newly re-formed republics are starting to run their own National Airlines with the old fleet.

Right: Manchester Airport is constantly introducing new measures and updating existing practices to combat threats to aviation security. Going through to a controlled area, everyone has to go through a metal detector gate and everything carried has to be X-rayed — all machines are film safe. Security equipment is the latest and most technologically advanced and the strong force of guards receive a rigorous and comprehensive training programme in line with The Department of Transport's stringent standards.

Bottom: Manchester Airport's baggage hall is equipped with highly sophisticated sorting machinery. Every piece of luggage is issued with a bar-coded label scanned by lasers which in turn cause actuators to direct luggage to the appropriate chute. It is then put on a waiting truck and driven to the aircraft.

Opposite: HM Customs and Excise officers work round the clock and are an essential element of Airport operations. One of their many duties is to prevent the smuggling of controlled substances, endangered species, diseased plants and the bringing of rabies into Britain. Part of the team is Bruno, a four-year-old black Labrador, seen here with his handler, Glen Whellams, who is conducting a routine search of an aircraft.

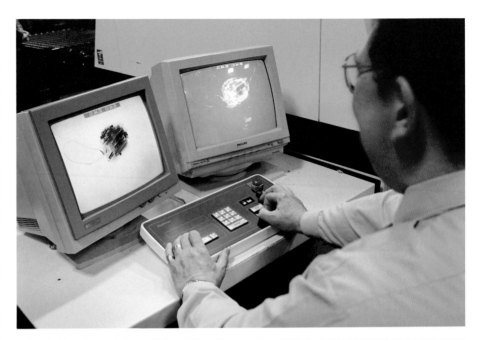

Below: Popular with both children and parents is the Playcare Centre in the international departure lounge. Currently sponsored by Vymura International Ltd, it provides toys, activity and fun — free of charge and supervised by qualified nursery nurses whilst parents can browse through the shops at their leisure or just have a few moments peace and quiet!

Right: Forte Retail Services' Tax Free Shop offers a wide range of luxury goods, photographic and audio equipment for the amateur or enthusiast and many useful items for the business traveller.

Below: Examining suspect luggage is part of routine duties for PC Paul Sadler (left) and PC Keith Mail who are among the 90 officers based at Greater Manchester Police, Airport, Delta West Sub-division. Police at the Airport have a special role to play in the prevention of terrorism, hi-jacking and extra security on high risk flights.

Right: An airport-hand from Ringway Handling Services loads a 'can' for a Britannia B767.

Below left: This ATI–Linee Aeree Nazionali DC9 is parked towards the end of the yellow line. Each aircraft type has its own pre-determined stop line, on this stand the furthest forward is for a B747.

Bottom right: Before departure a British Airways BAC 1–11 takes on catering requirements from the hi-loader on the left. These vehicles are designed to elevate all the way up to the main deck of a Boeing 747, some 5m above the apron.

Below right: A British Airways TriStar is refuelled before its journey to New York–JFK.

Opposite: The ground engineer walking with the Aer Lingus B737–500 is in contact with the crew to establish when they are ready to disconnect the tug.

Right: The impressive facility of FLS Aerospace Engineering stands on an area of five acres. The hangar itself, when completed in October 1989, was one of the largest in Europe, measuring a giant 26m high, 108m across and 104.4m in length. This gives a total floor area of 11,275 square metres (121,364 square feet). It can accommodate either up to two B747s or one B747 and two other wide-bodied aircraft, together with a number of smaller jets at any one time. Airlines from all over the world benefit from the specialist aviation maintenance, engineering and painting services provided by FLS Aerospace at Manchester.

Below: A newly liveried Eastwest Airlines of India B737, still with its British registration G–IBTX in the FLS Aerospace hangar.

Top left: The crew disembark to fight the fire.

Centre left: Firefighters attack the flames.

Bottom left: The aircraft is covered in foam to completely extinguish the flames.

Top right: Manchester Airport Fire Service use an old Trident aircraft in a remote part of the airfield to simulate fires and incidents as part of their rigorous training and practice drills. Here trays of fuel are set alight to simulate a wing fire.

Centre right: Dummies have been placed on board the aircraft which the firefighters have to locate and 'rescue' wearing full breathing apparatus.

Bottom right: Once rescued, casualty dummies are placed in the recovery position.

Opposite: Manchester Airport's Fire Service's four watches work twelve-hour shifts to provide mandatory cover 24 hours a day 365 days a year. This is one of two Marlin Foam Tenders, a high performer which carries 12,000 litres of water, 1,440 litres of foam and three crew quickly to any incident.

Below: During production of this book I was fortunate to be invited by Aer Lingus to see a pilot's eye view of Manchester Airport. In the cockpit of an Aer Lingus B737–200 Captain Fergus Ryan and First Officer Patrick Oliver approach runway 24 at Manchester.

Opposite: Manchester Air Traffic Control is one of the most up-to-date in the country. Controllers cover an area ranging from the Isle of Man in the west to Hull in the east, north to Carlisle and south to Birmingham.

Below: Forte Airport Services employs 700 people to produce between 140,000–160,000 inflight meals a week for 49 airlines. Head Chef Peter Wilson (left) discusses a dish with Chef David Tremills.

Opposite: In between flights this Convair 580 of DHL is parked on the West Apron in front of the World Freight Terminal.

Below left: The cargo is stored in racks awaiting collection by freight agents.

Below right: Loading up, an American Airlines B767 carries urgently required freight for the USA.

Opposite: Goods are transferred to the World Freight Terminal. Manchester's excellent location, served by a spur from the M56 affords quick connections to the M6, M62–61 motorways allowing freight to continue onward with ease. In fact Manchester is within two hours' drive of 60 per cent of the UK's manufacturing industry.

Below: A bus is loaded on to a Heavylift Belfast for export.

Opposite: The foreground shows some of the specialist lifting equipment used to load/unload the many types of cargo on to the different aircraft. The Federal Express B747 on the shot has brought racing horses from Wellington, New Zealand, to Manchester for training by Britain's top trainers. The aircraft is in the basic colour of its former owners, Flying Tigers, but carries Federal Express logos over the door.

Below: Aerospacelines Super Guppy being loaded with the first Airbus A340 wing manufactured in Chester by British Aerospace. It will be flown to Bremen in Germany for the fitting of flaps prior to being flown to Toulouse, France, the final assembly line for Airbus Industrie.

Opposite: Emery Worldwide operate a scheduled weekly flight from Brussels to Manchester and on to Dayton, Ohio. Here is one of their DC–8–73 freighters, an old design re-engined with new quiet and fuel efficient CFM56 engines.

Below: In the middle of the night, a side-loading Aer Lingus B737 freighter unloads items of clothing made in Ireland bound for the UK shops.

Right: Come rain or shine, the freight operation at Manchester takes place 24 hours a day, 365 days a year. An Emirates Airbus A300–600 being loaded up with freight for the Middle East.

Below: An Air Hong Kong B747 moves across a wet apron to runway 24. Air Hong Kong have increased the number of their all-cargo flights from Manchester to four per week.

Opposite: Named 'The City of Elgin', British Airways B747 to Islamabad takes on cargo.

Overleaf: This Southern Air Transport DC–8 on charter to Aeromexico is being loaded with NCR cash machines for use in Mexico City.